Giggles, Gags and Groaners

MAD SCIENCE
EXPERIMENTS

WRITTEN BY:

STUART A. KALLEN

Published by Abdo & Daughters, 6535 Cecilia Circle, Edina, Minnesota 55439.

Library bound edition distributed by Rockbottom Books, Pentagon Tower, P.O. Box 36036, Minneapolis, Minnesota 55435.

Printed in the United States.

Cover Illustration: Terry Boles
Inside Illustrations: Terry Boles

Edited By: Rosemary Wallner

Kallen, Stuart A. ,1955-
      Mad Science Experiments/written by Stuart A. Kallen
            p. cm.-- (Giggles, Gags and Groaners)
      Summary: A collection of simple experiments which are performed with common household items.
            ISBN 1-56239-128-3
            1. Science--Experiments--Juvenile literature. 2. Scientific recreations--Juvenile literature. [1. Science--Experiments.
2. Scientific recreations. 3. Experiments.] I. Title. II. Series:
Kallen, Stuart A., 1955- Giggles, Gags and Groaners.
Q164.K36 1992
507.8--dc20   92-14776
                                                                       CIP

AC
      International Standard   **Library of Congress**
      Book Number: **Catalog Card Number:**

      1-56239-128-3   92-14776

DISCLAIMER —The experiments in this book are meant to be conducted with relatively harmless ingredients. Abdo & Daughters is in no way responsible for persons or property harmed by the misuse or misinterpretation of any experiments, intentional or not.

Table of Contents

IT'S ALL AROUND US

Science. When some people think of the word, they think of long formulas, dry text, and strange laboratories. But science is more than test tubes, beakers, and droning professors. Science is fun! Everything around us is based on science. Inventors and scientific laws have built the wondrous modern world that we live in today. How does our bicycle go down the road? Science! How does our video game work? Science! Cars, planes, and trains? Science! Even the food you eat is brought to you by science. Science is everywhere.

In this book, you'll use simple household items to create science magic. Hidden in your kitchen, basement, and garage are dozens of tricks, stunts, and games based on science. If you follow the instructions in this book very carefully you can become a science magician.

Amaze your friends and family, learn something, and have fun. Some of the tricks in this book require scissors or other kitchen items. Please be very careful when using these items. Get permission from an adult before doing any experiments. Better yet, get an adult to help you.

When doing experiments, read through the entire description first. Next, gather all the ingredients together in one place. It is important to have everything you need on hand. Then, let the science magic begin!

LAUNCH A CORK ROCKET

You can't build a space ship in your backyard, but you can make your own mini-rocket out of a few simple items. When baking soda is mixed with vinegar, carbon dioxide gases build up in the bottle. Stand back and watch your cork rocket fly!

YOU WILL NEED:

•a tall soda or wine bottle

•a cork

•thumbtacks

•scissors

•colored construction paper or the Sunday comics page

•a measuring cup

•vinegar

•water

•a tissue

•a teaspoon

•baking soda

THE EXPERIMENT:

1. Carefully cut 4 paper streamers 1/4 inch wide and 6 inches long out of the colored construction paper or Sunday funnies.

2. Using the thumbtacks, attach the streamers to the end of the cork.

3. Fill the bottle with 1/2 cup of water and 1/2 cup of vinegar.

4. Put one teaspoon of baking soda onto the edge of a tissue. Roll the tissue up around the baking soda and twist the ends tight. (See illustration.)

5. Take the tissue and baking soda, the bottle, and the cork outside where you will have plenty of room.

6. Drop the rolled up tissue into the bottle. Put the cork on as tight as you can. It is important that the cork be on very tight.

7. Stand back and wait.

THE RESULT:

When the baking soda seeps through the tissue it will create carbon dioxide gas inside the bottle. When the gas builds up, the cork will shoot into the sky with a loud pop. This takes almost five minutes, so stand back. **Do not point the bottle at anyone or anything. Keep your face away from the bottle opening**. If you are patient, the cork rocket will make a loud pop and fly high into the sky.

AN EXPLANATION:

Baking soda is marvelous stuff. It is an important ingredient used in baking bread, cakes, and cookies. When mixed with other ingredients like milk or vinegar, baking soda releases carbon dioxide gases that make the baked goods light and fluffy. Because it is a fine powder, baking soda can also be used as a nonpolluting substitute for cleanser.

CONSTRUCT A
VIEW CAMERA

More than three thousand years before the camera was invented the Greeks perfected the camera obscura. Now known as the pinhole camera, camera obscura means "dark room" in Latin. With some simple items, you can make your own devise like the ancient camera obscura. You can view the world in miniature — and in living color!

YOU WILL NEED:

•a ruler

•a pencil, pen, or maker

•scissors

•an empty cereal box or laundry soap box at least 12 inches tall

•waxed paper

•a needle

•masking tape

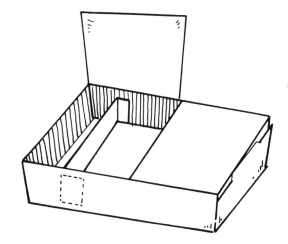

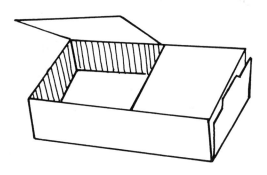

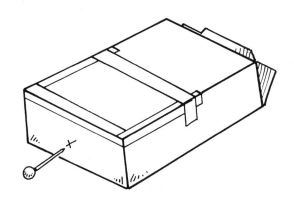

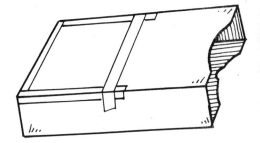

THE EXPERIMENT:

1. Pull the wax liner out of the cereal box and throw it away. If you are using a soap box, tap any extra soap flakes out into a sink.

2. Measure a distance of 5 inches from the bottom of the box. Draw a line across the box with your pen.

3. With your scissors, cut the box on the line. Cut from the line to the bottom of the box. Cut across the bottom of the box so that you have a flap of box that folds up on one side. (See illustration.)

4. Cut a piece of waxed paper the same size as the bottom of the box.

5. Tape the waxed paper across the box. It should go from side to side about 2 inches from the bottom of the box.

6. With the needle, punch a small hole in the bottom of the box.

7. Tape the flap of the box back into place. Make sure no light leaks in through the tape.

8. Cut the top of the box in a semi-circle that can fit around your nose and forehead. (See illustration.)

9. Stand in front of a window.

10. Hold the box up to your forehead and point the pinhole at a sunlit scene. If you don't see anything it is probably because light is leaking in around the tape or where the box is pressed against your forehead. Put a towel over your head and your camera to block out the light. But make sure that the pinhole is **not** covered.

THE RESULTS:

You will see a miniature color copy of the scene reflected in the box. It will be upside down on the waxed paper. If it is very out of focus the pinhole is too large.

AN EXPLANATION:

The camera obscura works in much the same way as our eyes. When we look at something, the light of the image passes through the tiny opening in our eye called the pupil. (This is similar to the pinhole.)

The image is "projected" onto the back of our eye where the brain "sees" it. Just like the camera obscura, when we look at something, it is reflected upside down in our eyes. Our brains switch the image right-side-up so that we don't walk around seeing the world upside down!

In ancient Greece people made pinholes on outside walls of darkened rooms. The scene from outside was projected upside down on the opposite wall. Artists sometimes traced the scene and then painted it on the wall.

Astronomers have used the camera obscura to project images of the sun, moon, and bright stars. Inventors put photographic film in a similar box and invented the camera.

CREATE A
BUBBLE FOUNTAIN

Here's another experiment with baking soda. Better do this one in a sink or outdoors. This experiment is messy.

YOU WILL NEED:

•a tall soda or wine bottle

•baking soda

•water

•liquid or powder dish or laundry soap

•vinegar

•a measuring cup

•a tablespoon

•a teaspoon

THE EXPERIMENT:

1. Add 2 cups of water to the bottle.

2. Put 1 tablespoon of baking soda in the bottle.

3. Put a few drops of liquid soap or 1 teaspoon soap powder into the bottle. Cover the top with your thumb. Shake the bottle until the soap is dissolved in the water.

4. Put the bottle in a sink or take it outside.

5. Pour 2 tablespoons of vinegar into the bottle.

THE RESULT:

A fountain of bubbles will flow out of the top of the bottle.

THE EXPLANATION:

This is another experiment where baking soda and vinegar release carbon dioxide gases. The action of the gas mixes the soap into a bubbling froth.

SET UP A
STAR PROJECTOR

This is a great way to shine stars on the ceiling or the walls of your bedroom. If you want to get real tricky, look up star patterns (constellations) in a book. Then you can make the Big Dipper or one of your favorite constellations.

YOU WILL NEED:

•an empty cereal box or soap box (a round oatmeal container works the best)

•a good flashlight

•scissors

•masking tape or any strong tape

•a pencil

20

THE EXPERIMENT:

1. Pull the wax liner out of the cereal box and throw it out. If you are using a soap box, tap out any extra soap into a sink.

2. Cut small star patterns in the bottom of the cereal box. If this is too difficult, use a pencil to poke small holes in the bottom of the box. If the holes are too big, your constellations will not look as good.

3. Cut a hole for the flashlight in the top of the box.

4. Tape the flashlight securely onto the box.

5. Turn on the flashlight in a darkened room.

THE RESULT:

You will see stars shining wherever you point your star projector!

THE EXPLANATION:

The light from the flashlight shines through the holes in the bottom of the box. The cereal box blocks out all of the light except where you cut your star patterns.

GROW A GARDEN
ON A SPONGE

Add greenery to any room with a sponge garden.

YOU WILL NEED:

•a sponge

•a small, shallow bowl

•grass seeds or any other small plant seeds; buy seeds at a hardware store, grocery store or plant store.

•liquid plant food (this can be bought at the same places as the seeds)

•water

THE EXPERIMENT:

1. Put the sponge in the bowl.

2. Pour enough water into the bowl so that half the sponge is covered with water.

3. Sprinkle seeds over the sponge.

4. Add water to the bowl every few days. If the sponge dries out, the experiment will not work.

THE RESULT:

Within a few days, you will see plants growing out of the sponge. Once the plants sprout, add a few drops of liquid plant food to the water. This will keep your sponge garden growing for a long time.

THE EXPLANATION:

Most seeds only need moisture to sprout. Since sponges hold water it is a perfect environment for the seeds to sprout. When plants grow, they get "food" from the soil. The sponge contains no nutrients. With a sponge garden, plant food is necessary to feed the plants.

MAKE INVISIBLE INK

Do you want to write a message that is invisible? No one will be able to read it. That is unless they know the secret way to make the message appear.

YOU WILL NEED:

• a lemon, orange, lime, or grapefruit

• a knife (BE CAREFUL!)

• a bowl

• a piece of typing paper

• a fine paint brush, Q-tip, feather quill, or a dried up pen

• a lamp

THE EXPERIMENT:

1. Put your hand on the fruit and roll it around on the table. After a minute it will become good and soft. This makes the fruit juicier.

2. Cut the fruit and squeeze the juice into a bowl.

3. Dip the brush, Q-tip, feather quill, or pen into the juice. Write a message on the typing paper using the juice.

THE RESULT:

When dried, the message will be invisible. To read the message, move the paper around very closely to a light bulb for a few minutes. When heated properly, the message will appear. The bulb is hot, be sure not to touch it!

THE EXPLANATION:

When the fruit juice is heated, it burns. When things burn they create carbon. The black smoke from a fire is carbon being released. When the ink burns, the carbon is left on the paper making the secret message readable.

MAKE ROCK CANDY

When you are done with this experiment you will have a treat to eat! **This experiment requires the help of an adult! Do not use the stove without an adult's permission!**

YOU WILL NEED:

•sugar

•water

•a measuring cup

•a long-handled spoon

•a saucepan

•a glass jar

•a pencil

•a piece of string

•a clean nut, bolt, or washer

THE EXPERIMENT:

1. Pour 1/2 cup of water in to a small saucepan. Bring the water to boil on the stove.

2. Slowly pour 1 cup of sugar into the water. Stir the sugar with the spoon until the sugar is completely dissolved.

3. Boil for one minute.

4. Pour the solution into a jar.

5. Take a piece of string that is as long as the jar.

6. Tie the string around the middle of the pencil.

7. Take the clean nut, bolt, or washer and tie it to the other end of the string. This will act as a weight to keep the string tight.

8. Put the pencil over the mouth of the jar so that the string hangs down in the sugar water.

9. Put the jar in a corner where it will not be disturbed.

THE RESULT:

After several weeks the water will evaporate. Sugar crystals will "grow" on the string. Be patient, this experiment takes some time. If you want to grow sugar lollipops, use a straw instead of a piece of string.

THE EXPLANATION:

Crystals are very pure forms of any substance. Many different solutions make crystals including baking soda and salt.
The sugar that we buy at the grocery store is ground up sugar crystals. In this experiment, we reformed those crystals.